"*Quarterback Management* provides a re[...] business management using a football gan.. .. .. a paradigm. It is a book worth reading and worth applying to create a profitable business. I would highly recommend it to managers and entrepreneurs who are thinking of starting a new enterprise."

—Benjamin M. Hawkins, dean at Lundy-Fetterman School of Business, Campbell University

"This book is an excellent guideline for successful business management. It has the basic fundamentals for growing your business on a solid foundation."

—Charles "Chick" Adams, retired entrepreneur, business owner, and former Duke University football player

"Having spent twenty-eight years in television sports, I have always known that the skills and talents needed in football are ironically identical to the ones that must be present if a company is to succeed. This is exemplified to perfection."

—Phil Stone, veteran sportscaster for NBC Sports, ESPN, Raycom, and Prime Ticket Network

"The game of football mimics life. The ups and downs on the playing field and in our lives emphasize the need to make good decisions. This book provides a game plan for that and more."

—Danny Talbott, 1965 ACC Football Player of the Year, University of North Carolina quarterback, All-American baseball player and thirty-three years in pharmaceutical business with Ortho-McNeil, subsidiary of Johnson & Johnson

"*Quarterback Management* provides nuts and bolts examples of how to apply basic success principals to a game plan for your business. It is a valuable read for new business owners and a good reminder for more seasoned businessmen as well."

—Scott Stankavage, University of North Carolina Quarterback 1981-1983 and Denver Broncos Quarterback 1984-1986.

QUARTERBACK MANAGEMENT

How to Call the Plays for Your Successful Business

Van W. Cuthrell

iUniverse, Inc.
Bloomington

Quarterback Management
How to Call the Plays for Your Successful Business

Copyright © 2010 Van W. Cuthrell

iUniverse books may be ordered through booksellers or by contacting:

iUniverse
1663 Liberty Drive
Bloomington, IN 47403
www.iuniverse.com
1-800-Authors (1-800-288-4677)

ISBN: 978-1-4502-8269-7 (pbk)
ISBN: 978-1-4502-8271-0 (cloth)
ISBN: 978-1-4502-8270-3 (ebk)

Printed in the United States of America

iUniverse rev. date: 12/16/2010

To friends and family who kindly gave support
and advice, this book is gratefully dedicated.

And to the memory of two wonderful business partners:
Charles L. Revelle Jr. and John R. Prince Jr.

Contents

List of Figures

Foreword

By J. Huntley Cuthrell

Having worked for twenty-five years in sales and marketing within the printing paper industry, I contribute much of my success to what my father Van taught me as a youth, and as an adolescent, and now as a middle-aged adult. I have lived my life learning how my father applied the principles he experienced while playing and coaching football to his experience as a manager and owner of his businesses. I have witnessed how these gridiron ideas weaved their way throughout business, bringing success no matter what the product or service. As a result, it excites me to write the foreword to this book.

It is my wish that the reader of *Quarterback Management* will benefit, as I have, by applying the winning principles of the Xs and Os in the game of football to his or her own businesses, and to his or her life, bringing championship results.

Preface

Football is a game designed to be fun for the participants. *Quarterback Management* is written to be a fun book, easy to read, with the emphasis on making managing fun. When you are having fun doing whatever it is you do, you are definitely being successful.

The Fighting Irish of Notre Dame achieved number-one status in football during the 1988 season after years of mediocrity and disappointing play. This return of prominence was achieved under the leadership of a 150-pound, five-foot eight-inch man by the name of Lou Holtz. Though small in stature, he is a giant among men. It took him three years to achieve this goal, and by his own admission, it was reached ahead of schedule. Lou Holtz was a leader with a plan. He operated with a short-term plan, a long-range plan, an annual plan, and a game plan that utilized his personnel to their best advantage. He left nothing to chance and reached his goals by exercising the best options available.

Quarterback Management is not about one individual, but it is about having a plan. It is not just about football but the need to have a plan, whether on the football field, in business or on life's playing field. It is about scoring touchdowns and the execution of a plan to do that, and making a profit in the business world. It is not about recruiting, but it is about hiring the right people. It is about scout reports and competition in business. It is about football practice and employee training. It is about championships, and it is about management leadership. It is about pride and team records and it is about winning with a plan.

The main purpose of *Quarterback Management* is to provide a general outline and guide for small business managers. It is directed to those individuals who find themselves in a management role not because they are Harvard Business School graduates but because they either inherited a management position in the family business or they rose up from the ranks. It is also directed to the increasing number of energetic entrepreneurs who have started, or plan to start, a new business of their own.

Managers often find themselves in situations they cannot solve. Too many times, a manager gets started with "seat of the pants" management and succeeds for a while in spite of himself. Managers experience growing pains, and therefore continuously seek solutions and answers to their problems. The fact is, at some point in time, a business and/or company must come to grips with some sound management methods, or it will never achieve its potential. Worse yet, it could be overtaken by a competitor. A business must have a plan. By incorporating sound management techniques into a plan, by following the plan, by monitoring it, and making necessary changes when needed, managers can lead a company with confidence and have fun while doing it.

The intent in *Quarterback Management* is to pass on to small business managers some of the simple management ideas and techniques that worked so well in our organization. By implementing these unique strategies and following our overall "game plan" we were able to enjoy many years of success in the steel building industry. They are not new techniques and ideas. There is no deep, dark secret we uncovered in our company. Rather, they were ones we adopted as a result of attending sales meetings and management seminars and gleaning common sense solutions to complex and everyday problems. Our very best answers were brought forth within the organization, born out of need.

There are too many owners or managers who put in long hours, are overworked, overwhelmed, burned out, and not having fun. They are so busy trying to manage chaos they cannot see the forest for the trees. These organizations amble along without direction. They operate on a day-to-day basis reacting instead of acting. They are totally content with mediocrity. They are boring and faceless companies in danger without realizing it.

If your company even bears a slight resemblance to this description, *Quarterback Management* is for you. Let's do something about it. Begin by accepting the challenge. Take charge of your destiny. Be the new starting quarterback and lead your team. Include your employees, challenge them, and encourage them to share your dream.

The Challenge

The United States Army had a slogan: "Be All You Can Be."
Former President Jimmy Carter wrote a book entitled, Why Not
the Best? Well, why not? You may never be the best tennis player
in the world, or even the best at your own racquet club, but the
chances of making your company the best in your city, county,
and state, in your particular industry, are probably much better.
Remember that only the game fish swim upstream.

I challenge you to think like a quarterback. Establish a "game
plan" and call the right plays. Be a quarterback manager. Guide
your team with the use of management tools and techniques that
are proven and sound, and become winners.

Let *Quarterback Management* help design a "game plan" for
your company. It need not be a specific goal. It should not be
based on such things as meeting quotas or deadlines. It should
entail a detailed plan that has vision and ambition to make your
company successful. Your plan should excite and motivate your
employees. It should solicit their support and involvement.

Use this book as a guideline, but develop your own plan.

Then constantly review it and revise it from time to time. But use it! Develop the most lean and efficient organization in your industry. You will achieve financial success, but that will only be the spin-off. You will be happier and have more time to enjoy other interests: your family and your friends.

CHAPTER 1
GAME PLAN

The ultimate objective in football is to move the ball across the goal line, but that can only be achieved if a game plan provides a means of getting it there, four or five yards at a time. The game plan must include a mix of running plays, short pass plays, down-field passes, etc. The 2009 Georgia Tech Yellow Jackets were very successful running the flex bone offense, winning the Atlantic Coast Conference championship in Coach Paul Johnson's second season. This type of offense is difficult to prepare for and gives opposing coaches fits. It is a very different plan and it works. Give credit to LaVell Edwards of BYU as the first coach to have a more dominant offensive passing scheme, which led to his team's 1984 National Championship.

Regardless of the specific game plan, one thing that must be present if the team is going to win is *execution*, which comes from good management and good leadership. It is the same in business. Good decisions will come easier if they are thought out in advance, one step at a time, rather than being spewed forth in a breathless ninety-nine-yard run for an elusive goal. In order for a game plan to work well in business as it does in football, we must first understand what management is all about.

The US Army has the best definition of leadership I have ever heard: "Leadership is the art of influencing and directing people in such a way as to win their willing obedience, confidence, and respect in order to accomplish a mission." One of the army's most famous leaders, Dwight D. Eisenhower, put it more succinctly after he became president: "You can't push a piece of string, you have to pull it."

I strongly believe that this simple definition of leadership applies to managing as well. Good management involves leading, not forcing. In football, the quarterback must be up front and must take charge, leading his team toward the goal. He can't push them from behind or give advice from the sidelines. As the quarterback is the leader on the football field, so is the manager the leader of the company—up front, engaged in the game, and confident in his ability to call the right plays at the right time.

Quite often, in my experience as a former high school coach, I observed players of average physical ability become great players because of their leadership qualities. They seemed to have that special knack for inspiring others. They demonstrated a tremendous will to win, and a strong sense of dedication and determination.

They also had the ability to convey these same emotions to the rest of the teammates.

Not everyone is a born leader. It is a rare person who reaches the pinnacles of success attained by Dwight Eisenhower, Bill Gates, and Peyton Manning. Great leaders seldom "fly by the seat of their pants." They are keenly aware of the importance of having the right plan and using it wisely to reach their objectives.

Many business managers have more of what it takes to be a leader than they realize. They are already armed with desire, enthusiasm, and the determination to reach their business goals. With a little help and the right game plan, such managers can achieve success on their own playing fields. In addition to providing leadership, the wise manager must also make the best possible use of his time and energy, and encourage others to do the same.

My college economics professor had a favorite saying: "Time is of the essence, young man." He repeated it over and over. He had no time for idle chitchat. By the time I completed his course, I had learned that lesson. Time is of the essence, and, of course, time is money. It always shows up on the bottom line.

A well-conceived game plan can help managers make the right decision and make it quickly, thus avoiding costly time-consuming debate over every new problem that arises. And the plan can help both managers and employees avoid mistakes that can be even more costly, and sometimes devastating.

In football, when the team is in the huddle, the quarterback always has a play to call to advance the ball toward the goal line. It is not a play created hastily in the heat of the moment. Each play is part of a careful game plan, a procedure that the entire team has practiced time and again. The plan is designed to do the following:

a. exploit the opponent's weaknesses;
b. take advantage of the team's own strengths;
c. utilize the position on the field;
d. take full advantage of the time left in the game; and
e. take into consideration the amount of risk to take.

These are just a few of the factors that can influence the choice of plays. But that decision has to be made in the huddle in a matter of seconds, and the play selection cannot be made with proficiency if the team does not already have a game plan.

The same principles apply in business, but managers have one great advantage over quarterbacks on the field. Managers normally have more time in which to call the play. It stands to reason that management decisions can be made with more precision and a better chance of success if there is already in place an overall business plan to follow in the same way that the football team adheres to its game plan.

Success in business flows from decisions based on action, not reaction. By having a plan, a manager can learn to trust his instincts. Ideas will take shape because the business blueprint is already laid out. The manager can perform like the quarterback who has practiced the play so many times he knows instinctively how to make the right choices.

In the vast playing field of outer space, astronauts have a game plan for dealing with various emergencies. Before a spacecraft is hurtled into orbit, the space travelers, and all their support personnel, have practiced, and practiced, and practiced. By following a plan formulated in advance to deal with all kinds of events, both expected and unexpected, these adventurers remain calm and cool in the face of situations that are sometimes life threatening. Because they know what needs to be done, and what can be done, they avoid panic and confusion, and concentrate on a proper course of action.

This has been so clearly shown to us in the January 2009 "Miracle on the Hudson" when US Airways Captain Chesley B. "Sully" Sullenberger safely glided his jetliner to a perfect emergency crash landing on the Hudson River in New York without the loss of lives. When asked to comment days later, he calmly stated that he and his crew were simply doing the jobs they were trained to do. His forty years of experience, preparedness, and training surely made a difference. There was a plan.

A well-thought-out plan can also take advantage of the wisdom gained through hindsight. In business, as in football, a game plan should provide historical data. It should incorporate past experiences that have been proved successful. In football, if a play is successful, it is used over and over. In business, if a certain promotional campaign has been successful, it can be used repeatedly, and a record should be kept to show results. This written "game plan" becomes a valuable source of reference at later times. If a play or a promotional campaign does not work, on the other hand, the record should show that as well.

As a senior playing quarterback at Guilford College in North Carolina, my coach wanted something different, some razzle-dazzle surprise for our big game against the leading team in our conference. Our scouts had noted that these opponents had excellent pursuit on kickoffs, so the coach designed a double reverse play in hopes of neutralizing their aggressive pursuit. When the big day arrived, we received the opening kickoff. I was the safety and received the kick running toward the right sideline and I handed the ball off to another back going in the opposite direction. He handed it off to another back going yet again in the opposite direction for a double reverse. As you might expect we were losing ground getting dangerously close to our own goal line. Our guy got hit on or near our goal line and fumbled the ball in our end zone and Lenoir Rhyne recovered for a touchdown! They kicked the extra point and the score was seven to zip and only seconds had run off the clock!

Before the second kickoff, I went over to the sidelines and asked, "Coach, do you want to run the double reverse again?" "Yes," came the reply. "Let's try it again." On the kickoff, our halfback carrying the ball got tackled in the end zone, giving the other team a safety! The score was now 9–0 and still less than a minute played in the game! After the safety, we kicked off and Lenoir Rhyne, on their first play from scrimmage, ran sixty yards for another touchdown. The score was now 16–0 and we had yet to run an offensive play!

I went to the coach with the question that was on everyone's mind: "Would we run the double reverse again?" The answer was short and clear. "Hell, no!" The double reverse was banished from the play book. It was a mistake our team would never make again. In business, as in football, a written game plan can provide a record that will help prevent costly mistakes from being repeated.

Is a game plan all there is to operating a business? Follow it, and it's a done deal? If that were true, businesses could proceed like robots depending on rote memory to get them from one day to the next. Of course, that is not the way it is. With the most comprehensive game plan, there is still plenty of room for spontaneity. The plan is a guide and a source of reference. It provides direction, invites innovation, creative thinking, and decision making that is consistent with the company overall goals.

In the following chapters, you will learn how you can formulate a game plan to cover all aspects of your business … from hiring and training to marketing and profit margins. A plan, which if tailored to your situation, can enable you, as a manager, to achieve your business goals and be successful.

Ask yourself the following:

1. Will I use *Quarterback Management* and other sources to improve my leadership skills?

2. Will I set the example as a good time manager and encourage others to do the same?

3. Will I be more proactive anticipating opportunities and problems in order to have a game plan dictating *action* rather than *reaction*?

4. Can the goals of a football plan, as described, be applicable to my future plan for my company?

5. Will my plan provide critical historical data that will lend itself to increased confidence in making decisions?

CHAPTER 2
GAME PLAN FOR HIRING

When you talk about real estate, location is the key. When you talk about success in a business enterprise, having the right people is the key. In a nutshell, your employees are extremely important and can give you a substantial competitive advantage. It's amazing to me that most managers would agree with that statement and yet do little about it. Hiring the right people is hard work. And it should be, because it is the most profitable thing you can do for your organization. The greatest coach in the world cannot have a winning program if he doesn't have some talented players.

A local businessman once gave me the highest compliment I could imagine while I was coaching high school football. He said, "You seem to place your players at the right position for which they are best suited, and then get the maximum effort from them." Well, that wasn't pure luck. My coaching staff worked very hard trying to match our players with the various jobs on the team. We not only matched their skills to these positions, we matched their personalities as well. After all, the talent and mind-set needed by a quarterback is quite different from what is required by a linebacker.

It is imperative as a coach to understand the physical skills, the mentality, and the personality needed for every position on the team. Quickness drills, speed trials, and strength and agility tests can help him determine where a player excels, or fails, in physical ability. But it requires a keen observation to determine the personality traits required for these positions. Some of my best players were not the ones with the superior physical skills, but they achieved through hard work, discipline, and great attitudes. The desire to win, to be enthusiastic, and to overcome adversity is of utmost importance for success. A winning football coach must constantly look for these intangible traits in every one of his players.

The formula for selecting the most qualified players can work in the business world as well as on the football field. Yet some managers select their employees with no plan at all. The idea is to have a detailed job description for every position. You must know what characteristics, intelligence and skills are required for that position. This information will not only be helpful in selecting new employees, but it will aid you as well in making promotions from within. Never overlook present employees in an effort to fill new positions. One of the best salespeople I ever hired started out as an administrative person. She was an asset I almost overlooked, but given the opportunity she really performed.

Usually, the interviewer of potential employees scans a resume, asks a few questions, which probably have already been answered on the application form, and then proceeds to do all the talking, leaving the applicant to mutter or nod in agreement at appropriate times. The decision to hire is then based on a "gut feeling" influenced, perhaps, by the candidate's dress code or physical appearance, and, of course, that resume. I have never seen a bad resume! An applicant may be attractive and nicely groomed and might make a favorable first impression, but does that mean he or she can do the job? What about ability? More investigation is needed to more fully determine if the candidate is the best person for the position.

We once interviewed a college professor for a sales position in our company. I had been favorably impressed with his resume. The first interview had gone well as his credentials were impeccable, and he was very articulate. After testing him, however, using nationally recognized materials, we found his scores to be disappointing in several of the categories. He scored far below average on mechanical comprehension and mathematics. In fact, he scored below the median on every test we administered. Since he was a college professor, I had assumed that testing would be a mere formality. If we had not had in place a hiring plan, which included testing, I would have made a terrible mistake. I would have hired him based on a gut feeling, an accomplished resume, and a favorable first impression, and I do not think either of us would have been the winner.

A hiring plan should consist of at least three interviews, depending on the position to be filled. I call the first interview "Let the applicant talk." Ask questions about the resume, and be certain you thoroughly understand statements about experience, education, and references. Be courteous in asking questions, and above all don't do too much talking. Encourage the applicants to talk about themselves by asking a few personal questions about his/her likes and dislikes. This approach usually reveals much about the applicant's attitude and character. And remember your job in the interview is to listen, observe, and be keenly aware of everything the candidate says and does.

The second interview is the "Testing" interview. Here the objective is to measure aptitude and basic skills. Testing should tell you if the skill levels of the applicant are equal to the task … a very important point. A poor math score would not bode well for a prospective bookkeeper or purchaser, for instance. Human resources consulting firms offer batteries of tests that can be of use to your particular company and industry.

If your candidate has been successful through the first two stages, the following sessions should deal with terms, policies, and expectations. Getting to this point assumes, of course, that you are satisfied with your own investigation and the references from past employers, colleagues, associates, or fellow workers. Bear in mind that such comments generally don't mean too much since the applicant would not give you a bad reference.

If you do a thorough job of interviewing, it is my strong contention that it will pay off tenfold in the end. The time you spend interviewing could be the most valuable time you could ever spend with this person. If you make a mistake here, it will prove costly to everyone. Finding the right person can be an agonizing process, but you simply cannot allow yourself to settle for a "warm body."

It is also a good policy to involve the candidate's prospective supervisor in the interviewing process. You don't want to wait for the new employee's first day on the job to find out there is bad chemistry between these two people.

Finally, if everyone in your organization is overworked and you desperately need help, you must be careful not to give in and hire mediocrity. If you have a hiring plan and are committed to it, you will persevere and be happy with your ultimate choice.

A prospective employee may be intimidated by your hiring plan. I frequently heard this comment: "I've never been through such an extensive interview." This emphasizes the need to explain to the prospect that the intensive procedure in the process will help ensure, "You are right for us and we are right for you!" It was always interesting to me that, after this explanation, the more worthy candidates wanted to "make the team" even more. They sensed that this company expected more than mediocrity and that, if selected, they would be part of a winning team. If workers start out with, and maintain, this attitude, you will notice that your employee turnover rate will be very low.

In addition, job candidates should know when they are hired that there will be periodic reviews for job performance. And you, as manager, owe it to your new employee to do just that.

When you are diligently searching for that right person and it seems like it is taking forever, keep in mind that the effort you make in the hiring process will save enormous time over the long haul. Employees will be happier and will remain loyal through the ensuing years.

I once interviewed eleven secretarial candidates before I found one who got beyond the first interview. All the prospects had decent resumes, but only one had the necessary credentials to get to the second interview.

Applicants interviewing for sales or engineering positions in our organization were required to have their spouses join them for the final interview. Quite often, our key people put in more than forty hours per week. It was imperative that we not hire "clock watchers," and it was also important that the spouse understood all aspects of the job and would be supportive. The inclusion of the spouse at the interview is not uncommon with large corporations, nor should it be with your company.

Sometime during the interviewing process it was my practice to have lunch with the candidate. I had a real "hang-up" about hiring anyone who was an excessively slow eater. It has always been my observation that a person who takes forever to eat is slow about everything and lacking a sense of urgency. Maybe I was a little too harsh about this.

The last financial officer I hired reminded me, before my retirement, of the day he was hired. He said, "We met for lunch at the Lucky 32 restaurant." "Yes," I said, "I remember it well." He went on to say, "We both ordered a small side salad with our entrees, and when I finished my salad I noticed that you had already finished your entire meal. Knowing what I now know about your reputation of not hiring slow eaters, I wonder, 'How did I make the team?'"

Believe me: I worried about his slow eating that day all the way back to our office. The final interview that afternoon went very well. I reasoned that if he was to be the keeper of our money, I wanted him to be extremely cautious and accurate, slow eater or not! He proved himself time and again.

Do you have to pay the highest salaries to get the best people? Probably not. So what does it take? You have to show applicants that they are joining a winning program. And they need to know they will have the opportunity to advance within the company. They should understand that they will be given responsibilities and that you pay and promote employees according to results and not years of service. This is how the good college football recruiters sign the best talent year after year. The recruiter sells his program to the athlete and assures him that he can contribute and reach his personal goals as part of that program.

This does not mean that you oversell your company. Just be honest and tell the bad with the good. Here again, the most common mistake managers make in the hiring process is that they talk too much. Don't be guilty of overselling yourself or your company. Remember your basic role as the interviewer mentioned earlier in this chapter.

Think what would happen if you hire people who are 5 percent smarter, 5 percent more enthusiastic, 5 percent more dependable, who have 5 percent more energy and 5 percent better attitudes than your competitor. What will this do for you? Your employees will be 5 percent more productive, and ultimately, put 5 percent more gross profit on your ledger sheet! And you will find you have 5 percent more time for yourself!

An intensive hiring plan such as the one I have discussed may sound selfish, but it is really a win-win situation for you and your employees. They will learn to respect you and they will appreciate the fact that you try hard to secure competent people who will contribute to the team effort, and in doing so make everyone's job easier. Individuals might score points, but it's the team that wins the game!

The key people in our company consisted of sales personnel,

engineers, project managers, assistants, receptionists, a financial officer, superintendents, foremen, and assistant foremen. We were always looking for good people, and we were very much aware that our growth was almost totally dependent on hiring competent employees.

At this point, you may be thinking that your situation is different from mine. It really doesn't matter whether you run a bakery, a clothing store, a nursery, or a plumbing supply business. You still have employees. The key is to get that competitive advantage by hiring the very best people available.

Now, as the manager, you might say to yourself, "My employees are all in place. I don't need to hire anyone." But the question you should be asking yourself is this: "Are they in the right positions? Are they happy with the role they are playing? Are they effective and productive?"

Test your current employees, if for no other reason than to have some comparisons for future reference. If you are satisfied with the performance of a current employee and need to hire someone for a similar position in the future, it will be helpful to have this information.

Be certain that your testing procedures are commensurate with the positions you wish to fill. Remember, the skills required for a warehouse superintendent are not the same as those needed for a sales position.

This chapter on selecting your "players" may be the most

beneficial and important chapter in this book. If you don't have the right people, the progress of your business will be limited. It is absolutely imperative you develop a "game plan" for hiring. This plan will take the worry and anxiety out of hiring and provide a check and balance for that old "gut feeling." Use the plan diligently and you will find you don't have to settle for mediocrity.

Let's think about some ideas for a game plan that will help you hire and promote the right people for your organization.

1. Draw an organization chart of your business showing names, titles, lines of authority, brief job descriptions, and proposed new jobs.

2. Create a file on each employee with a detailed job description and a brief evaluation of each employee's strengths and weaknesses. The file should include your personal updated assessment of each one as to ability, attitude, personality, maturity, tolerance, and appearance.

3. Make a personnel forecast. List your anticipated personnel growth for the next twelve months. Indicate the month the employee may be added and be sure to start your search well in advance.

4. Conduct a proper and extensive interview to be sure you hire the best person available. Remember, if ten people apply, don't just hire the best of the ten. If no one truly qualifies, start over from the beginning.

Use the following as a guideline for interviewing:

1. Use a proper application form to screen the applicants to be interviewed.

2. In the first interview, or "Let the applicant talk" interview, remember to be a good listener, but be sure to ask any questions that might give a clue to character and attitude.

3. The "Testing" interview should be conducted only if the applicant passed the first interview with flying colors.

4. At the Terms, Policies, Expectations sessions, you should, at this point, be favorably impressed and want the candidate on your team. This interview is meant to relay the hard facts about your expectations, presenting the bad with the good. Have the spouse present and include the person who will be the applicant's immediate supervisor for at least part of the interview. Let the supervisor participate with questions and answers.

Ross Perot, the Texas multimillionaire who founded Electronic Data Systems and later sold it to General Motors, once said, "Eagles don't flock. You have to find them one at a time." Develop a hiring plan, be patient, be thorough, and find those eagles. They *are* out there!

Ask yourself the following (use the spaces provided below for your comments):

1. How do my hiring practices compare?

2. Have I been diligent enough in the past in hiring new people?

3. Because it is hard work finding good people, have I accepted mediocrity?

4. What is my employee turnover situation?

5. Do employees leave because of money or something else? Do I make an effort to find out why they leave? Did I perform an exit interview?

6. Am I always looking for that "diamond in the rough"? If not, why not?

CHAPTER 3
GAME PLAN FOR TRAINING

You have been through the hiring process, and you are confident you have hired the right person. The new employee is reporting for work Monday morning. What next? Do you have a plan for training this new person on your team?

Too often a manager drops the ball here and leaves a new employee to fend for himself. The manager tends to feel the task is over, thinking, "I've hired this new person and now I can get on with my normal work." Not true! A manager must never fail to realize the importance of making a new employee feel like part of the team as soon as possible. The manager needs to have a prior meeting with all other employees and motivate them to assist in bringing this new person along for the good of the team. Everyone needs to realize that a new environment represents a tremendous adjustment for the new person, and that helping with this adjustment will prove beneficial for all.

At the outset, it is critical the "new kid on the block" is properly introduced. A group meeting with all employees with whom this person will be working is a good idea. It is necessary for the new employee to understand, at least in general, every player's role and responsibility to the total company effort. In addition, this explanation of the various employees' responsibilities will give a manager an excellent opportunity to praise his staff. It is a great time to show appreciation for the contributions that the team players make. A manager should never miss the chance to display the confidence and respect he has for all current employees in front of the new person. It will serve to reinforce the decision of the new employee that he has, indeed, joined a winning team. This "introductory approach" will also eliminate the potential fears of any of the current employees that may be intimidated by a new face on the team. They will have been praised by the manager and will appreciate that they have been solicited to help with the training process.

These techniques about which I have written—introducing a new person to the other employees—may sound trivial and unnecessary to some of you. Others would think all managers would know to do these things. But that is not the case. Think back to when you were a new employee. Was your adjustment to the new environment easy? And how long did it take before you felt like a member of the team? Could management have done a better job helping you through this period?

A thorough job description should have been prepared and presented during the interviewing process. A training program designed to prepare the new person with the skills needed to meet the job description requirements is the next objective. All of us find it much easier to operate if we know what is expected of us. Every football player has a job description. The players are given a play book which describes the responsibility for every position and every play in the book. The responsibility may be the same or similar for more than one play. But every player has a little different assignment for each play. Can you imagine the chaos if there was no job description for football players?

Let's assume that your new employee is going to be in sales, and you are expanding your business by adding a new salesperson. The job description will be pretty obvious. The salesperson is to match your company products with customer needs in such a way as to gain complete customer satisfaction, and to make a profit for the company. The objective here is to basically have every sale be beneficial to the customer, as well as to the company.

The training of your new employee should include the following:
1. Product knowledge
2. Competition
3. Pricing policy and terms
4. Time management

5. Responsibilities of other employees

6. Role playing

Start your training with product knowledge, and provide everything possible for this endeavor: literature, videos, discussions, demonstrations, and your own PowerPoint presentation. Help your trainee learn to overcome objections. Teach him/her what questions to ask when determining the true needs of a prospective customer.

It is important that your sales trainee knows about the company's competition before he faces it head to head. He must know the competition's strengths and weaknesses. He should know what differentiates his own company from these competitors, and be able to communicate this information to a prospective customer with conviction and sincerity.

Your new employee will have to understand your pricing philosophy, terms, and company policy concerning every possible contingency involved in a sale. He must also know how much latitude he might have as to pricing, policy, and terms.

Time management is probably the most important aspect of sales training. It is like teaching someone how to study. If you had good study habits in school, chances are you never had to worry about good grades. The salesperson who has learned to manage his time will never have to worry about sales quotas! Almost every salesperson will have product knowledge and awareness of competition. What differentiates the "peak performers" from the "also-rans" are the ones with a game plan for managing their time. It is so crucial.

In our company, "role playing" was the final training session for new sales personnel. It should only be done after the other aspects of training have been mastered. For us, role playing was intense as we tried to come up with every conceivable scenario. The customers in our role-playing sessions were full of questions and objections that presented a tough challenge for the sales trainee. This difficult challenge, and thorough practice, prepared the trainee well for the game. The confident graduate of our role-playing sessions was eager to get into action. He would be prepared and ready to present a sales game plan which consisted of a well-rehearsed, step-by-step, give-and-take procedure designed to satisfy customer needs and ultimately get the sales order.

On one occasion, we had a new salesman sell the first two prospects he visited on the very first day out on his own! He had been well trained and obviously satisfied the customer's needs. This person later became the nation's top salesperson for selling Butler steel buildings to the agricultural community in the late 1970s. He sold over one hundred buildings in a single year. That equates to two buildings per week. The second highest salesman was also on our staff! Let me point out that these are not the ten feet by twelve feet small storage buildings you find in the backyards of suburbia. These are the 2,000- to 5,000-square-foot maintenance shops and equipment storage buildings found on farmsteads across America. To my knowledge, no one has ever surpassed the records set by these two peak performers!

As a manager, it is your responsibility, and obligation, to train your new person thoroughly and well. Give the trainee a set of plays just as a quarterback uses plays, and teach him/her to execute the plays to perfection. Encourage new salespeople to read self-help books. Train them in taking notes, remembering names, telephone manners, email etiquette, and other techniques. Advocate becoming good listeners and, most importantly, teach good time management.

The training should be ongoing and include outside sales seminars, self-improvement courses, such as Dale Carnegie, technical training to stay abreast regarding product knowledge, and any other support available to make them feel confident and proud to be in sales.

How many times do you hear managers say the following? "The last salesperson I hired just didn't work out. He went six months without selling anything." Chances are the manager did a poor job selecting this new salesperson and did an even worse job with his/her training. At the same time, managers need to be patient and not expect miracles.

In my thirty-six years of experience, we never hired a person for sales we had to dismiss. They all became productive, and proved profitable for us within six months. Maybe we were just lucky. If you will develop a good game plan for your hiring procedures, and then train the new person properly, perhaps you will be lucky too.

As training is the foundation for success on the football field, it is also the formula for success in the business world.

Ask yourself the following (use the spaces provided below for your comments):

1. Do I have a job description for every position in my company?

2. Do I make proper training of new employees a top priority?

3. Do I monitor the progress of new employees and encourage feedback?

4. Am I a good listener when I do get feedback?

CHAPTER 4
GAME PLAN FOR INCENTIVES

Hopefully, at this point in your reading, you are seeing the great advantages derived from having a plan for every facet of your organization. When you, as the leader, begin to express enthusiasm and commitment to a game plan that is shared by your employees, you will begin to see some positive changes in your people. This sense of job security for you and your employees will be enhanced when everyone realizes that tomorrow does not have to be like yesterday. We can, and will, improve our performance and competitive position in the market place.

Your enthusiasm for a game plan will be contagious, but you will also need to provide some innovative perks and incentives to get the ball rolling. Everyone likes to be a part of a success story. Solicit the help of your employees and together set some realistic but attainable goals both for the short and long term. Challenge your personnel to be peak performers. Give them responsibility with accountability. Help your people develop pride in team performance and the good feeling of being part of a winning tradition. You can accomplish these things by having a game plan for incentives.

Incentives can take on many faces. Incentives can be bonuses, promotions, trophies, trips, and prizes. The key to incentives is to make them meaningful and appropriate for each particular employee. Every key person in our company had some type of incentive, and we had a strong incentive program.

Let me take you through a review of our incentive plan. Maybe it can help you, as a manager, to create a plan of your own. Our greatest incentive program was designed for our sales staff. Our sales staff was paid a base salary with all expenses, an automobile, and an escalating sales commission based on the volume of sales. I must admit that the salespeople were the "prima donnas" of our company. But we firmly believed that nothing happened within the company until the sale was made. It was what made our world turn.

We were highly dependent on our sales force to convince customers we could provide the best possible product and service. We were probably the most sales-oriented farm-building company in America. Since we demanded much from these people, they were paid well and were provided with many perks. For example, all of the salespeople who made their quota in sales were invited, along with their spouses, to the annual franchised dealer meetings (or conventions) which were held at various resort areas throughout the country. These meetings were held in places like Las Vegas, New Orleans, San Francisco, Phoenix, Orlando, and Hawaii. These events were most welcomed and anticipated every year. What do you think this did for morale?

The monetary incentive for our support people was always based on volume. If we had a high volume of sales, it naturally increased the workload of the supporting staff. Each support person, administrative assistants, and project managers would get a percentage of the volume based on what we felt was fair for that particular position of responsibility.

Can you imagine, therefore, how everyone in the company was glad to see the "prima donnas" come in with a sales order? Touchdown! Everyone was happy! The salesperson got a pat on the back from the entire staff. The support people were like the linemen on a football team congratulating the running back for crossing the goal line.

The salesman was like the running back giving credit and praise to the lineman for making it possible. It was teamwork in action everywhere. And all brought about by incentives.

Repeat business represented about 40 percent of our sales every year. Satisfied customers are the easiest to sell. Therefore, in order to increase, or add, to our customer base, we introduced another incentive technique in which we gave our salesmen an additional bonus for new customers every month. It is always easier to make calls on an old customer, one who already knows your name and game. However, it takes an extra effort to get that new customer. It means an effort that requires making a cold call, making a good first impression, giving a super presentation, and doggedly staying after the business until the final sale is made. This incentive obviously benefitted both our sales force and our company. As the sales base grew, the pyramid got taller … more prospects raised their hands, and we ended up with more repeat business.

Another incentive was provided for the construction foreman who directed and supervised the erection of buildings in the field. We kept job-cost records. If the foreman came in under the job cost, he shared in the savings. A review of the job cost was done every month with the foreman and the manager. This job-cost review served not only as an incentive for the foreman, but it also pointed out if our labor-selling prices were realistic. In addition, it allowed the manager to evaluate the productivity of different work crews and the foreman since many jobs were identical.

Pay incentives for the foreman had quarterly draws. But half was retained to be paid at the end of the year. The retained amount was only paid if that particular employee was still on the payroll. In other words, the money was not paid to anyone who quit during the year. The company workload was heaviest from April through October, and anyone leaving during that time really put an extra burden on the other employees. Obviously, this pay-incentive program worked for the company in that it kept the team intact during the busiest time of the year.

The large bonus checks awarded to employees at the end of the year often provided down payments on new homes, new cars, home improvements, and other large-ticket items. It proved to be a welcomed "forced" savings account for some. It was a particularly satisfying experience for me to present these checks to well-deserving employees.

Another very important pay incentive was the annual Christmas bonus. Our Christmas bonus program was for *every* employee and was based on longevity and attitude. Attitude carried the most weight.

Many times during the year management observed an extra effort on the part of a particular employee. Our quarterly meetings provided management the opportunity to recognize this special effort, and it was followed up at the end of the year in the Christmas bonus. There was a maximum limit on the amount of Christmas bonuses awarded. It was not unusual for a lower-paid employee to receive a Christmas bonus equal to that of the star salesperson.

Our company hosted an employee appreciation dinner annually. On this occasion five-, ten-, fifteen-, and twenty-year plaques were presented to the employees, along with checks varying in amounts according to years of service. This gave management an excellent opportunity to recognize, thank, and praise individual recipients, *in the presence of their peers.*

Everyone is not motivated by money. I have had a hard time realizing this, but it is true. Recognition, praise, and a sincere "Thank you" go a long way with many people. Still, other employees would rather be rewarded with a day off or two, with pay, to go fishing or hunting or shopping. Others would prefer a weekend retreat with their spouse, and/or family or friends. Sometimes this more personal approach is much preferred over the monetary way. It says, "I care and appreciate you and what you do for the company."

Being flexible with your incentives is good, but it requires effort on your part, as the manager, to know what really motivates each individual employee. If you can empathize—walk in his shoes—you will learn what that "hot button" really is and push it!

As you can see, our company was extremely incentive orientated. We strongly believed incentives promoted teamwork and built morale. I believe it is an effective way to hold employee turnover to a minimum. Incentives worked for us, and they can work for you too. Incentives can be utilized in any type of organization, and they can be implemented for all employees, in some form or another. It is a management technique that should be incorporated into every company's game plan. The results of such a plan can have very positive effects on employees, and definitely have long-range benefits for the company. As a manager, you will want to be creative and innovative in designing incentives for your own staff that can be meaningful and rewarding.

One final word of caution regarding the development of your incentive plan: think it through thoroughly, and be absolutely sure you are not setting a precedent that you cannot live with in the future. Nothing could be worse for morale than to start an incentive program and then have to end it. However, please do not let this be a deterrent to initiating a program that will benefit your company and your employees.

Incentives are good things. They say if you work hard, you will be rewarded. High school football teams have incentives—conference championships, state championships, all-conference teams, all-state teams, potential college football scholarships—that could provide opportunities otherwise improbable. On a higher level, college players have these same opportunities when successful in the form of bowl games at resort cities. If they are really good, they might get a chance to play on Sunday. This level is where the air is really thin. As my good friend Pete Winstead would say, "Many come but few qualify."

Ask yourself the following (use the spaces provided below for your comments):

1. Do we have enough perks or incentives for our employees?

2. Have I given proper thought to what motivates every individual and particularly the key players?

3. Have I been innovative enough?

4. Do I assume everyone is motivated by the same stimuli?

CHAPTER 5
COMMUNICATION WITH
TEAM MEMBERS

Open channels of communication between employees and management is vital to every successful business. A successful marriage is based on good communication between a husband and wife. Just as there must be give and take in a marriage, there must also exist in your company a two-way form of communication between management and employees.

A manager must include in his overall game plan avenues of communication for his company. The quarterback communicates with the team in the huddle, and you, as manager, need to communicate with your people on a daily basis. It is necessary for you to exchange information with them, if you are to be successful. If you are not communicating with them, they cannot possibly know what your expectations are. If they are not communicating with you, you cannot possibly know what their needs are, or their capabilities, or their full potential.

Communication within the organization will make you aware of team morale. Team morale is of the utmost importance to any company, and unfortunately one of the things most often overlooked. As a manager, you cannot simply assume that everything is going smoothly with your employees. Most morale problems can be resolved easily, but knowing they exist is the hard part. Managers tend to keep their heads in the sand and do not realize the importance of employee morale.

My experience proved that keeping people informed did the most to hold down morale problems. False rumors can ruin an organization. Every effort should be utilized to keep the "record straight." If you plan to make a change in company procedure, explain it to your employees and tell them why it is necessary. Solicit the support of your people when a change is to be made. If the support is not forthcoming, there is probably a very good reason for the lack of it. When you ask for answers or suggestions, and you don't get any, you can be certain there is a problem and you need to do something about it.

Communication within our company came about in several ways. Let me share with you some of the techniques we used to encourage communication; then, perhaps it will aid you in developing your own.

There were the usual memos and daily verbal communication,

but in addition there were mini-meetings, which were meant to be brief, and our quarterly meetings. The quarterly meetings lasted from three hours to all day. They involved the key people of the company, and always included lunch together. The general procedure was to update our progress for the year, comparing it to our goals and objectives set for the year.

Each person was required to set personal goals for the next quarter, and to review his or her previous goals of the last quarter. These meetings were always productive, and everyone looked forward to them. It seemed, if our ship was getting off course or if we were dead in the water, these meetings served to get us back on course with sails trimmed and a fresh puff of air to get us going again. If there was a problem in sales, the production people were made aware of it, and often had good suggestions. If there was a problem in production, the sales force could learn to empathize.

Occasionally, these discussions became a little heated as everyone was encouraged to express themselves openly. There was one thing we did not allow: the meeting could not be a session for gripes or complaints. If there was a problem, we encouraged suggestions, but only positive and productive ones.

Employees were always made aware that mistakes can, and will, happen. If you were a decision maker, you knew you could make a bad one now and then. Employees were encouraged not to dwell on mistakes but to fix them. They were encouraged to help develop programs or procedures to prevent that mistake from happening again.

Any conceived idea was listened to no matter how "off the wall" it might sound. Our discussions were about any problem or opportunity that might involve employees, customers, competitors, or suppliers. We encouraged specifics, not generalities; fact, not fiction. A head football coach never wants to be told by an assistant that it is third down and one if it really is third down and two! You cannot make good decisions if you have bad information.

If morale was reported not to be good on one of our construction crews, we sought to find out which crew, what men, and why. If a competitor was really tearing us up on price, we checked to see how often. Three times? Ten times? What jobs? How much? If a supplier was long on delivery, we asked how late. Was it becoming a habit? Could we tolerate it? Whatever the problem, a plan was made to correct it, or improve it, and someone was designated and made responsible to take action within a certain time frame.

Mini-meetings that took place between the quarterly meetings also reflected our attitude of being positive and productive. Brevity was encouraged. In some of our mini-meetings, the participants were asked to remain standing. This way it underscored the meeting was meant to be brief. Many such meetings were called to "plant a seed" to be discussed at length at a later time after everyone had time to give it proper thought. Quarterly meetings and mini-meetings kept us on target with regard to the overall plan of the company. Most importantly, they provided a means to communicate.

One of the toughest jobs in our organization was that of our construction foremen. These men, and their respective work crews, often reported for work before sunrise, and because the job site might be fifty or sixty miles away they did not return to the office until after dark. This was particularly true from October through February when there was a limit of daylight hours. In addition, these men had to endure some pretty tough working conditions since their work was predominantly done outside. There were some very cold, damp winter days and some very hot, humid summer days. The foremen had to be innovative in order to keep morale from sagging among their crew members.

As a manager it was important for me to keep "my door open" to these foremen whose leadership was truly challenged at times. My foremen and I had many "father and son" sessions, as I called them. Their problems were my problems, and it was a challenge for all of us. But for all these laborious sessions, I always knew that when a foreman left my office, he definitely felt better if for no other reason than he had had an opportunity to be heard. I listened and tried to empathize. These foremen became almost like sons to me, and I truly knew they were strong spokes in the wheel of our company. They were like the linemen on the football field that do all the blocking. Our foremen were the guys in the trenches, the blood and guts guys, the unsung heroes. They definitely would qualify for the "All-Madden Team!"

It was always important to me to visit with my employees in their work place, and not just in my office. How could I "walk in their shoes" even a little bit if I did not occasionally visit that job site fifty or sixty miles from the office, and witness firsthand the ninety-eight-degree heat? It surely meant something to our guys when I would drive up with some ice-cold drinks and suggest we all take a break under the nearest shade tree and talk.

It also helps to know as much as possible about the families of your employees and staff, and to show a genuine interest in them. It is vitally important for you to know your employees' "hot buttons." It is vitally important that you know what turns them on, what motivates them, and what is important to them. The informal chitchats with my employees over the years proved to be some of my fondest memories of my business life. Remember, in order to motivate, you must first be able to communicate.

I recall one communication situation while playing college ball. It was a preseason practice and we were having a live scrimmage. My offensive right guard had been missing his assignment on several plays and as a result I was getting hammered pretty well. I was sacked or harassed on every passing play. You must remember this was before coaches started protecting quarterbacks in practice. I was getting very frustrated and really mad about what I thought was a poor effort on his part. So in the next huddle I slapped this player on the helmet and said "Hey, you play quarterback and let me block for you." He pushed me out of the huddle and took a swing at me and I tried to retaliate. He was a lot bigger than me and I was glad that the coaches put a stop to that fight before he hurt me. But, you know what? After that, he blocked much better and we left the field that day laughing about the incident. Sometimes, you just have to clear the air.

Communicating on the football field has changed drastically in the past several years. We now have coaches with headsets in box seats high above the field talking with players on the field. We have referees using instant replay to review calls. In business, we have technology that allows for much quicker communication between employees and externally with customers via email, Internet, etc. However, this can be overdone and place too much stress on everyone involved. Set some guidelines as to how you should communicate in the most practical and productive way.

Ask yourself the following (use the spaces provided below for your comments):

1. Do we have a plan for communicating with employees on a regular basis?

2. Just because my office door is open, do I assume my employees will knock, and do I encourage them to do so?

3. Do I make efforts to visit my employees in their workplace and try to walk in their shoes?

CHAPTER 6
COMMUNICATING
WITH CUSTOMERS

The previous chapter dealt with the importance of creating channels of communication between you, the manager, and your employees. Equally important is the need for an avenue of communication between the customer, or end-user of your product, and your company. Even if you are a manufacturer and never have the opportunity to see the customer, there should be some communication from him in regard to his acceptance of your product. Some of the finest products on the market today are the result of a customer's suggestion. Whatever the organization, a plan should be in place designed for customer contact and feedback.

The plan should entail contact during and after a sale, and should provide for the development of new customers. In addition, it should have a controlled method of constant contact with the customer. The more personal it can be the better. Let me explain again by revealing our game plan and techniques we used to enhance customer communication.

Our company was a dealer for Butler Manufacturing Co. of Kansas City, Missouri. For many years Butler was the leading steel building company in the world. The words "Butler Buildings" were synonymous with steel buildings. I was privileged to serve two terms on Butler's Agri-Dealer Council. This twelve-member board represented three hundred or more dealers throughout the country and provided feedback to Butler. The council met twice a year with Butler's top management, including the president and chairman of the board. They solicited our advice, and the advice of the dealers we represented in our local regions at home on policy, product development, and pricing. These meetings were usually three days long and were always productive. The council members were customers of Butler Mfg. Co. and, believe me, they listened to what we said, and they responded in a positive manner. It always impressed me how well they listened, and how hard they tried to solve the problems we faced as dealers. If I had to describe Butler Mfg Co. in one word, it would be integrity. It was a professional company and definitely customer oriented.

From my experience on the Butler Dealer Council, I decided to develop our own Customer Council. Since we served twenty-five counties in North Carolina and Virginia, we selected one customer from each county to serve on this council. Our salesmen made the selections and tried to choose a good cross section of our customer base, and not just our biggest customers. It was not a "structured" council with officers and designated meeting dates but served as our "in-house" contact for feedback and suggestions. The contact came about with a personal visit or a phone call. These "special" customers served as a sounding board for our company, and always appreciated the fact we solicited and valued their opinions. Our ties with these customers were strengthened by this approach, and they were most helpful. Particularly, they were helpful in advising us of new products we needed to consider offering for sale.

For your own business, you may want to consider a similar approach to customer communication. The more one-on-one personal contact, the better it is. You will be amazed how your customers will cooperate with this approach and will even begin to see your side of a problem, should one arise.

Another successful technique we used for customer contact and communication was a newsletter. The newsletter was sent out three or four times a year, and not on any specific date or schedule. It was sent out only when we felt we had something that needed to be conveyed to our customers. It was never more than one typed page, and it always contained a self- addressed, stamped return card soliciting their comments. The same approach can be done through email as well.

The newsletter typically included helpful information about

maintenance issues on equipment purchased from us, or simply to make them aware of how to get in touch with us for weekend service needs. Employee promotions within the company were given, and the names and brief biographies of any new employee added to our staff were also included in the newsletter.

The mention of any special pricing or discounts was also present, but in a low-key manner. The mailings were sent to 3,000 customers, and potential customers as well. This method of customer contact was extremely effective and served to make the customer feel a closeness to the company. Our customers were given every opportunity to be familiar with the names of all our personnel, and not just the salesman who called on them. We wanted our customers to know and depend on our entire team.

You may want to consider a similar method of communication. If so, let me make a few suggestions:

1. Be brief. A drawn-out letter or email is as boring as a long speech.

2. Have something to say that will definitely benefit the customer.

3. Make it as personal as possible. People still want that personal touch.

4. Make the customers feel that they too are members of your "winning team" and that you appreciate their business.

You might be saying at this point: "All well and good, but I'm just starting a business and I don't have a backlog of customers. I don't have a mailing list." Well, what is it they say? Necessity is the mother of invention. Let me tell you of a need our company had and how it came about for us to decide to expand our mailing list; to go out and find new prospects.

It came about after we had been in business approximately ten years. Business was particularly slow that year and we just did not have enough prospects. Salesmen, as a general rule, dislike making cold calls (calling on prospects who have never seen them before). It is the least desired part of their job. It is so much easier to return to a customer they have dealt with before, and, hopefully, find a need to sell more of your product. Cold calling takes more preparation. It's risky. Rejection comes quicker. Developing prospects by making cold calls is definitely unpopular. However, it has to be done in any sales-oriented company, and with the slow year we were having, we needed to be proactive and get something going.

We decided to canvas every county in our territory of North Carolina and Virginia. Our long-range plan, or goal, was to drive down every highway, every back road, and every dirt path and knock on every door of every prospect that might be in need of a steel farm building, grain bin, or irrigation equipment. Our short-term goal was to cover four to six counties in a year. It became a team effort, and everyone got his turn to be a team leader. The "lead" salesman could pick a county within his territory and the other salesmen, and myself, as manager, were obligated to set aside three to five days, over a two-week period, to canvas the area of that particular county assigned to him.

The team leader provided maps and travel directions and sales literature and brochures to be passed out to each new prospect. At the completion of the canvas, each team member had to write a report furnishing the names, addresses, and telephone numbers of all new prospects who he/she called on, and any other pertinent information. These names were immediately added to our newsletter mailing list. We always managed to get some immediate prospects and business. In time, many of the other contacts became customers also. Cold calling became fun for us! Isn't it always easier to endure an unpleasant task when you can do it with another person, or as a team? The plan worked so well for us that whenever things got a little slow, salesmen would often say, with enthusiasm, "Let's do a canvas!"

The program took about six years to accomplish and it established for us a mailing list and customer base unequaled in the industry. The company enjoyed enormous growth during that period of time. It was the most important step we ever took to ensure success. It was done without expanding our staff, and without spending any additional advertising money. It provided a "quick fix" for a salesman who needed a boost in sales. We had a game plan, and when things got slow we executed it. It was an idea born out of need. Again, like a pyramid, add to the base and the apex gets taller!

Another example of customer contact came about immediately after the customer signed a contract, and paid a down payment. The salesman responsible for the order immediately notified the erection superintendent for a spot on the erection schedule. This was followed by a letter from the erection superintendent to the customer introducing himself and thanking the customer for his business. In addition, he informed the customer of his role in the company, and assured him he would get quality workmanship. I believe this procedure served to reassure the customer he had made the right decision, and that he would be dealing with a company of integrity.

The need to communicate is vital for success. Keep your employees and your customers informed. Don't just promise. *Deliver.* Never disappoint them.

Let your customers know of your successes. People like to deal with successful people; it's human nature. People like to do business with someone who has a plan. They like to do business with a company they know will be around next year, and the next. They like to be included or involved in plans. Make your customers feel as though they are part of your family. Communicating with your customers makes them feel good too. It's a competitive edge in your particular industry that probably is grossly overlooked.

Check into it and begin now developing your communication "game plan," and take the lead among your competitors!

Ask yourself the following (use the spaces provided below for your comments):

1. Do you have a plan for communicating with your customer, or end-user of your product and/or service?

2. Do you have a plan for extending your customer base, or growing the pyramid?

3. Do you have a unique way of saying "Thank you" or showing appreciation for your customers' business, a way that differentiates you from your competition?

CHAPTER 7
WINNING BY MAKING A PROFIT

Throughout the book, we have discussed the importance of selecting the right players for the team, and the necessity of playing them at the right positions—employees being your players at this point. We have talked about the significance of training and that training should be ongoing. We have stated how vital it is to keep the players motivated with proper incentives. And we have elaborated on the importance of communicating with the players and the customers.

Now it is time to develop the game plan for game day. It is now time for strategy, and the formulation of a coaching philosophy that all the participants understand. You must communicate this basic plan so that you and your players/employees have a course of direction to follow in achieving your goals.

In the game of football, the objective is to win by scoring more points than the opposition. In the business world, the objective is to win the game by finishing the fiscal year with a profit. Profit is *not* a dirty word. Making a profit is absolutely necessary for a business to survive. A profit must be obtained without sacrificing the good will of the customer. In order to make a profit, you must have adequate margins. You must control your costs, and operate efficiently. In order to win on the football field, or in the business world, there must be a plan.

In football, there is a basic team plan that is designed for the season. There is also a game plan developed for use from week to week. It is formulated by watching film of the upcoming opponent and from studying scout reports.

In the corporate world there should be an annual business plan. This plan should incorporate the ideas and suggestions from as many employees as possible. The plan should include ongoing sales training, and a marketing and pricing strategy that will enable you to get adequate margins. The plan should assist with cost control and efficiency. It should also provide a method for evaluation of key competitors.

Margins: The First Key to Profit

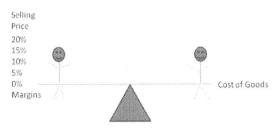

Figure 1

There are a number of factors that affect profit, but the first is adequate margins. What items influence margins? I believe there are many. Some are tangible, but many are intangible.

Let's list a few:

1. Image

2. Reputation

3. Sales philosophy

4. Sales staff

5. Competition

6. Profits

In Diagram #1, you see a seesaw showing the selling price on one side, and the cost of goods or service on the other. Let's first discuss some of these positive intangibles and then see what happens when you place these intangibles on the cost side of the seesaw.

1. Image

I believe there is a direct relationship between the selling price of your products and the image of your company. I am sure you will agree with that statement, and also agree that any improvement of that image will enhance your chances for a better selling price. To be successful, you must first "look" the part. That does not mean your facility has to look rich or expensive. It simply means that you must project the "image" that is right for success. Your company is what your customer, or prospect, perceives it to be.

One of the more financially successful people I know is an antiques dealer who operates out of an old barn. Although he could afford a much nicer building, an old barn is the image he wants to portray. He believes that his modest facility implies bargain prices and that a nicer environment might drive some customers away. On the other extreme, who has the nicest building in any town or city? Not just in my town, but in any town in America? It is the financial institutions! Who would dare put their money in a bank that looked anything less than the best?

Many times the first impression is the last one. You, as the owner or manager of your organization, should make every effort to ensure that this first impression is a good one. Take a long look at the physical surroundings of your work place. Does it project an image of success? Does it project what you think it should? What about the image projected by an incoming phone call, an email, or on your website? Are your employees polite and courteous? Are they friendly? Are they trained to repeat the name of a caller? Do they work at remembering the names of customers? Unfortunately in today's world you do not always get an employee answering a telephone. Often it is an automated recording with a menu of choices. Does this create a negative or positive image?

Image is so important, but not just the physical aspect. In the small town where I used to live, there are two hardware stores. One is much larger with a more attractive building. It has a larger inventory with lower prices. The other is just the opposite. But the smaller, less attractive, and more expensive store got my business because its employees were more friendly, more knowledgeable, and more eager to serve the customer. These people helped me solve my problem. They offered advice. I was not left to wander the store, pick something off the shelf, pay the cashier, and leave the store hoping I had the answer to my need. Just like me, customers like to be assured they have made the right decision, no matter how small or large. The "image" presented by this store was of good customer service.

2. Reputation

Your company image is what someone perceives it to be. But once your company has made a transaction with a customer, then that image becomes a reputation. Your reputation is on the line all the time—your company reputation for keeping your word, being dependable, and for being fair and honest. And it must be defended day after day by all your employees.

3. Sales Philosophy

We probably all agree that image and reputation are important intangible factors that affect company margins or profits. What is your sales philosophy? How do you and your sales staff feel about selling? Are you proud to be in sales? Do you display that pride? Isn't your attitude (and that of your staff as well) also an important factor? Let's think about this a bit.

How would you answer if someone asked, "How many salespeople do you have in your company?" If you have a total of thirty employees in your company, then your answer should be thirty because every one of your employees is a salesman if he/she has any contact at all with a customer!

Are you totally aware that nothing happens in a business until the sale is made? You can manufacture all the products you want, or provide all kinds of services, but until that product is sold, or services are ordered, no one gets paid. If selling and sales are what makes the world turn, then why is there such a negative attitude or stigma against salesmen? I suppose the distrust of salespeople comes about because there are, indeed, too many bad salesmen. When I made my decision to leave teaching and coaching and enter the business world, I was very reluctant to get into sales.

I have since learned that it is not only financially rewarding but also a lot of fun!

A carefully planned, step-by-step procedure, designed to culminate in the signing of an order or contract, can be an actual work of art. Think of it. Reread the sentence. It reminds me of a football game in that every well executed play takes you that much closer to the goal line. It can be exhilarating when you finally score that touchdown. And, like the game of football, when you are able to excel against the toughest of competition, that is when you enjoy it the most. Dispel any negative stigma you might have concerning selling, and encourage your sales force to be proud of being professional salesmen.

4. Sales Staff

How do you recognize the "professional" salesperson? Believe it or not, he or she has that special look of confidence and success. In most industries, 20 percent of the sales force sells 80 percent of the product or service. This 20 percent represents the true professionals. Why is this so?

Contrary to popular belief, they are not "born" salesmen. They work at it diligently. They are, first and foremost, time managers. They realize that "time is of the essence." They follow a plan. They know that efficiency means as much in selling as it does in manufacturing a product. They see more customers, make more presentations, get more leads, and close more sales because they use their time efficiently.

They realize, to some degree, that selling is a numbers game. Accomplished salespeople learn to scrutinize their time (as to priorities). The professional salesperson focuses his attention on one opportunity at a time, but he also knows it ranks at the top of his list of priorities. The real pros regard time as a precious commodity and will never waste it … neither theirs nor yours.

They exude confidence, and their enthusiasm for work is contagious. They infectiously command the respect of their fellow workers and customers.

In addition to being good time managers, the top 20 percent are organized and positive people. They handle problems expeditiously and get on to the next job at hand. Needless to say, they have to be good decision makers. Decisions are made only after studying all the facts. The top 20 percent use this skill in guiding prospects into making comfortable decisions of their own. They are very much aware they must assist customers in decision making, and then assure them that they have made the right decision. A good salesman knows the customer has to feel good about his decision … tomorrow!

Good salespeople are unique. They are fun to be around and interesting to observe. In our organization, we had a salesman who was a master at closing orders on Fridays. He would work on several projects for several days and try to reserve Friday for the final presentation and the signing of the order. He firmly believed that customers were more willing to sign orders on Friday because they were looking forward to the weekend. Customers wanted to be able to relax and enjoy the weekend without any unfinished business to be concerned about. This salesman's energy level, his enthusiasm, and his charisma were all in high gear on Fridays. It was without a doubt his most productive day! And don't you know he always enjoyed his weekends too?

Years ago, Union Camp Corporation of Franklin, Virginia, was one of the largest paper-manufacturing companies in the nation. They had a unique policy for greeting visiting salesmen. When a salesman entered the reception room of their offices, he/she was given a sheet of paper that read as follows: "Welcome to Union Camp Corporation. We want to extend to you every courtesy possible. We appreciate your calling on us and we appreciate you as a salesperson. We, too, have salespeople out in the field and know very well their importance to the success of our company. If there is anything we can do to make your visit with us more pleasant, please make your request."

Union Camp Corporation has since been bought by International Paper Company. I hope International Paper Company continues today this courteous greeting to all visiting salespersons because it is a winner. It shows that they do care and respect every salesman that enters their offices.

As managers, we don't like to be bothered by salesmen that

come in our door without an appointment. But courtesy must prevail. If you do not have time to spend with the salesperson, send him or her away, at least with a good feeling about your company. It will be to your advantage.

A technique we often used in our organization when greeting customers or salesmen coming to our office by appointment for the first time was to put their names on display prominently as they entered the lobby. Dale Carnegie was right when he said a person's name is the sweetest sound on earth to an individual. Seeing his name in bold print prominently displayed with the word "Welcome" is certainly impressive to the caller. I know of a college football coach who utilized this technique in recruiting football players. He would take a candidate on a tour of the campus, which, of course, included a visit to the stadium. Guess whose name appeared on the scoreboard?

Proper margins are vital to success, and the realization that intangibles, such as image, reputation, attitude toward selling, and all others we have discussed, are important and will enhance your chances for proper margins.

Look what happens to the seesaw when you add some of these positive characters to the cost of goods. Your selling price increases.

Figure 2

Sell the product, don't give it away! This must be your creed. Your sales staff and your total organization will only be as good at sales as you want them to be. A proper sales philosophy will benefit the whole company just as a proper coaching philosophy benefits the whole football team.

Another way to help your margins is to get the absolute best price possible for whatever it is you have to *buy* for your company or *resell,* be it vehicles, tools, equipment, furniture, or whatever else.

Americans are either too rich, mentally lazy, or both when it comes to negotiating. In Europe and other parts of the world negotiating is an economic way of life. As a good business person, you need to get your attitude right and start negotiating for everything you buy for your company. Every dollar you save goes on the top. Every dollar saved is, therefore, net profit. How often do you ask for a better price for an item? How often when you ask are you actually offered a better price? Does it hurt your feelings if you ask and don't get a better price? Are you wounded or insulted? You shouldn't be. The seller is counting on the fact that the American public does not like to be told "No!" The seller knows Americans don't like rejection.

In general, salespeople make terrible buyers. In our organization, I assigned someone other than me or a salesperson to do the buying. We needed someone who was more frugal than we were. There is no telling how much profit this person made for our company simply because he was a tough negotiator and very persistent at getting the best price for a product we needed. Our suppliers had tremendous respect for this individual and regarded him as a shrewd but fair businessman.

Be innovative with your buying strategy. Discuss with your suppliers every possible scenario for reducing the price. If you cannot get a better price, get better terms. Learn to say "No" to the seller, and know that time is usually on your side. Do not be afraid to spend money to save money. Take advantage of volume discounts.

Review your expenses for the past year and take an in-depth look at those costs that seem to be excessive. Solicit suggestions from employees regarding expenses. Make everyone aware that it is increased company profits that salary increases and bonuses come from, and that they can contribute to profits by helping to control expenses.

Just as there is a need to have a plan for every other aspect of your business, there must also be a plan that addresses your cost of doing business. The plan must deal with the factors that influence your cost of goods, and more importantly the efficiency of the total operation. This plan must be communicated and emphasized to the other employees on a regular basis. Never assume that your employees totally understand profits, but use every opportunity to make them aware that salary increases, perks, bonuses, and even job security come from company profits.

Let's take a look at what happens to margins when positive factors, such as efficiency and cost controls, are added to the seesaw. Your selling price goes even higher.

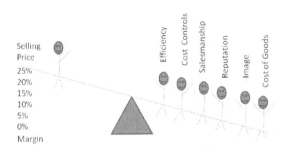

Figure 3

5. Competition

Without the presence of competition, there exists a monopoly. The few industries that exist as monopolies are mostly government controlled. Our democratic system has government agencies in place to protect the consumer from monopolies, and price fixing is totally against the law. If you are in a position to have a monopoly on a product or service, do not worry—it will not last long. Someone will eventually show up as your competitor!

When you say that you believe in capitalism, then your

next statement should be that you also believe in competition. You *welcome* competition. It's the American way. Life would be dull without it. Develop a positive attitude about competition. Competition is healthy because it provides the consumer with options. You, as a manager or owner, must not let competition dictate your company policies. You must have a plan for dealing with competition. Let's look at some aspects of a plan.

First, know your opponent. Know his strengths as well as his weaknesses. Study his pricing strategy. Keep records and notes of every confrontation or dealings that you have had with each other. Always assume when dealing with a prospect that there will be competition. If you do not know who your competition is, find out! Seek to know what his reputation is. Does he give good service? Is he honest and reliable? Do not react to his policy and procedures, but make your opponent react to yours!

Never call your competitor by name in the presence of your customer. Exploit his weaknesses by reference only. If you talk about your competitor, it will only give him credibility. If you practice all week on your "defense" trying to stop your opponent's "offense," then your own offense may go lacking. Work hard to ensure that your strengths outweigh those of your opponent, and that your shortcomings are not as great.

When coaching high school football, my game plan was to neutralize the other team's strengths. For instance, if they had an outstanding defensive lineman, our plan was to run hard right at him. If needed, we used two players to block him, but we ran at him. We did not shy away. This did two things: it gave our players the challenge to take on the opponent's best players. If it worked, as it almost always did, it proved to be very demoralizing to the opponent to see us gain yardage over their best guy. Secondly, it gave our players that extra bit of confidence that often separates the winners from the losers. The fact that we challenged our players made the difference. We chose not to run away from the opponent's strength, but to meet it head on, and defeat it.

How should you treat your competitor? Invariably, you will encounter your competitor at a trade association meeting or even somewhere socially. Treat him as a friend. Think about this: if he is good at his job, you might want him on your team some day. Be positive about your business and industry, and encourage him to talk. Remember, be a good listener. You will not learn anything from him if you do all the talking. Be very courteous and never give him any reason to think of you other than the gentleman or lady that you are. Keep your best foot forward just as though you were with a customer.

The art of intimidation is always at play in any competitive environment. The high school football team that I coached had certain drills and disciplines that were meant to intimidate the opposing team. For instance, we, the Red Devils, would take the field on game day in our white uniforms and red helmets and perform pregame calisthenics that had the precision of the

82nd Airborne drill team from Fort Bragg, North Carolina. The precision movements and cadence by which this activity was done were very intimidating to our opponents. Further, it was no accident that our larger and more athletic players occupied the front line nearest the opposing team! The art of intimidation— can it be used with your competition?

Acknowledge that competition is helpful. Don't be afraid of it. It makes a better player of you in your field of business. Again, let me emphasize: do not become so engrossed with your competition that his policies make up your policies and run your business. You be the leader and let him follow you. Be ever mindful of your competition because he, and only he, stands between you and the goal line!

6. Profits

You cannot be everything to everybody. You cannot give the very best service and have the lowest price. You cannot sell the highest quality product at the lowest price. What is your game plan regarding price? Are you going for big volume with a sacrifice on the price? Or will you sell less volume with greater emphasis on service and quality, but with higher margins? Certainly, these are things to think about when determining your pricing strategy. Both policies can be profitable, but you must decide what is best for you, and go forward.

Our company's strategy was to provide the best possible

service and product at a price that was generally higher than our competitor. We went for the "quality" image. We cost more, but we believed in the "we are worth it" approach. We tried to stay competitive and that meant our price was no more than 5 to 10 percent above our competitors' prices. We depended on our sales staff to convince our customers we were worth even more than that.

It is imperative that you know how your competitor is pricing his product. (But, here again, under no circumstances must you allow your competitor to dictate your pricing policy. If you do, you will find yourself going broke faster than he!)

There may be times when you seriously question the prices of your competitor. And it may concern you greatly if he sells his product much lower than you. But remember the bottom line is *profit*. Your competitor cannot survive if he does not make a profit.

There is a little restaurant in Virginia I have visited quite often over the years. I used to plan my sales calls with the idea of having lunch at this restaurant whenever I was in the area. It was always crowded. I had to plan on being there early, or it would mean having to wait for a table. The food was excellent, the service was good, and the price was unbelievably low. The last several times I was there, I noticed the trim on the building needed paint, and inside the restaurant the furniture and carpet showed excessive wear and tear. I remember thinking that if the owner would raise his prices 5 to 10 percent, he could afford to keep this restaurant in good condition. I was convinced he would not lose a single customer by doing so. I concluded that if he continued to operate as he was, he would eventually find himself in a catch-22. His business would go down because his facility was deteriorating, and if he waited too long to be proactive, his customers would not be willing to pay higher prices to eat in a dump! It would become a no-win deal for everyone.

Take a look at your pricing strategy. Review it often. Stay abreast of your competition. I am not suggesting you take advantage of your customers in your pricing, but do not wake up one day and find you are in big trouble because you sold your product or service too cheaply!

Ask yourself the following (use the spaces provided below for your comments):

1. Can I improve my company image?

2. As a manager/owner, do I communicate to my employees the importance of first impressions?

3. Is our reputation discussed at every opportunity?

4. Is my sales staff proud to be in sales? Do I, as their manager/owner, make them feel proud?

5. Do I encourage and demand professionalism of my sales personnel?

6. Do I constantly seek ways to improve the continuous training of our sales force?

7. Do I give them all the tools they need to do a good job?

8. Do I know my competition?

9. What are his greatest strengths?

10. What are his weaknesses?

11. Is our company the leader in the industry? If not, do I have a plan to be the leader?

12. What is our pricing philosophy?

13. Do we let our competitors dictate our prices?

14. How often do I review our pricing policy and our prices?

CHAPTER 8
GAME PLAN FORMAT

We've talked enough about having a game plan. Let's now get involved and actually develop an outline for your company's game plan. It should be long-term as well as immediate. The long-term approach should be sound with great regard for the general ups and downs of your industry. The document should provide you with the following:

1. A process to evaluate where your business is today.

2. A path for you and your employees to follow for the next twelve months.

3. A plan to use with financial institutions to justify needed capital.

4. A communication tool with employees that will ensure a mutual understanding of everyone's goals and objectives.

5. A plan that ensures that the short-term plan supports

the long-term plan and is realistic, attainable, and can be measured for results.

Mission Statement

Develop a clear, simple statement that defines the purpose of your business in detail. Ask yourself, "What business am I really in?" Your mission statement should address the markets that you hope to serve, the products and services that you hope to sell, the overall purpose of your business, and the factors that differentiate you from your competition. The following is an example of a mission statement. It is the mission statement developed and used by my former company.

> Our company mission is to sell and erect steel buildings and grain bins serving the agricultural and light industrial community with a "turnkey" approach.

Describe your mission statement.

Marketing Plan

A. Local market. Describe your local market in terms of geographic size and population, and other factors that you consider important.

Example from my former company:

> The local market is considered to be seventy-five miles from home base since this is the maximum distance we can send our crews to erect with any real efficiency. There are approximately 1,000 medium to large farms located in this area. Additionally, there are at least 2,500 small businesses in the same area that have a potential use for our products and services.

Describe your local market:

B. Business climate. Evaluate the general business and economic situation in your area. Provide a one paragraph summary of your local business climate.

Example:

> The agricultural situation is getting better after some very difficult years. Our efforts should be directed toward the larger farmers and to the small businesses that require a simple "plain vanilla" type steel building.

Describe your business climate:

C. Market opportunities. List any market segments that have provided profitable opportunities for your business.

Example:

1. Large commercial peanut storage bins and buildings.
2. Large commercial grain storage.
3. Farm shops (farmers have a need to be able to repair and service their own equipment).

Describe the market opportunities of your business:

D. Competition. List the four major competitors in your market area. Describe the strengths and weaknesses of each competitor along with the products and services they provide.

Example:

Competitor #1:	ABC Builders
Product and Services:	Pre-fabricated steel buildings with a "turn-key" approach.
Strength:	Low price, attractive building and fair reputation.
Weaknesses:	Not active twenty miles from home base.
	Not as much sales oriented as mechanical.
	Does a poor job of promoting products and services.
	Does not have a strong professional image.
Marketing Rating:	A very distant second to us in the areas in which we are both active.

Competitor #2:	Stick Builders
Product and Services:	Pole barn builder.
Strength:	Lower price, if customer does not require a slab foundation.
Weaknesses:	Quality does not compare with an all steel building.
	Cannot meet the building code requirements in many of the areas we work in without getting out of line on the price.
Marketing Rating:	Fourth and declining.

List the four major competitors in your market area:

Competitor #1:

    Products and services:

    Strengths:

    Weaknesses:

    Market rating:

Competitor #2:

    Products and services:

    Strengths:

Weaknesses:

Market rating:

Competitor #3:

Product and services:

Strengths:

Weaknesses:

Market rating:

Competitor #4:

Products and services:

Strengths:

Weaknesses:

Market rating:

E.   Market standing. State how you view your company position in the local market relative to your competitors.

Example:

> Very strong. We are definitely the leader in our area selling farm building, grain bins, and center-pivot irrigation.

State your view of your company position in the local market.

F.   Competitive strengths. Describe the areas that clearly distinguish you from your competitors. Indicate how you will capitalize on your advantage.

Example:

1. Historical reputation. We have been in the business longer than any competitor and enjoy an excellent reputation for customer satisfaction. We continue to advertise that fact.

2. Stability. We have been able to endure the ups and downs of agriculture and maintain a very low employee turnover rate.

3. "Turnkey" approach. From site preparation to the finished product. Not every competitor has that capability.

Describe your company's competitive strengths.

1. Historical reputation.

2. Stability.

3. "Turnkey" approach.

G. Weaknesses. List the primary weaknesses of your business.

Example:

> Because of our long history of selling buildings on the
> farm, we are not identified as commercial or industrial
> builders.

List the primary weaknesses in your company.

H.   Sales strategy. Briefly describe your ideas for getting your
     share of the market.

Example:

> Direct mail campaign to all top farmers on our mailing
> list. Personal contact with all commercial grain and
> peanut buyers in our territory. Price advertise buildings
> in major newspapers in territory.

What exactly is your idea for getting your share of the market?

I.   Advertising strategy. Outline your local advertising strategy for the year. List the different types of advertising that you will use and show the percentage of your total advertising budget that will be spent on each type.

Example:

    Direct mail, newspaper, radio, newsletter, website, yellow pages, and television.

Outline your local advertising strategy for the year.

J.   Customer satisfaction. Describe the actions you will take to address customer needs, and focus on long-term customer satisfaction. Indicate how you intend to measure customer satisfaction.

Example:

1.   Make an in-depth evaluation of customer needs.
2.   Design buildings or systems to fit those needs.
3.   Provide service after the sale.

4. Have personal contact by sales personnel with customers during the construction phase.

5. Have a six-month follow-up with customers regarding degree of satisfaction.

Describe the actions you will take for customer satisfaction.

PERSONNEL PLAN

A. Organization chart. On a separate sheet, draw an organization chart of your business showing names, titles, lines of authority, and proposed new positions.

B. Human resources. On a separate sheet, provide a short biography of each employee. Include a brief evaluation of each employee's strengths and weaknesses.

C. Personnel forecast. On a separate sheet, list your anticipated personnel growth, by employee classification, for the next twelve months. Indicate the month or months that new employees may be added.

D. Employee training. On a separate sheet, outline your proposed training program for the new year.

E. Employee turnover. Describe how you plan to minimize employee turnover in your business.

Example:

> Install some incentive programs designed to increase business and boost morale.

PRIORITIES

On a separate sheet, list the ten most important action items or activities that you plan to accomplish in the next twelve months. Name the persons responsible for each action item and the time line for its start and completion.

Example:

Action Item	Persons	Time line
1. Reduce the man/hrs required for construction	Ted, Eddie, Wyn	Nov. 15 – ongoing
2. Increase the number of cold calls	All sales personnel	Nov. 15 – ongoing
3. More frequent visits to job sites	All sales personnel	Nov. 15 – ongoing
4. Review construction pricing	Ted, Joseph, self	Dec. 15th – 22nd
5. Rewrite terms in contracts	Arden, self	Dec. 15th – 22nd
6. Plan advertising campaign in detail for next year	Ted, Beth, self	Dec. 15th – 22nd
7. Evaluate bonus plan for erection foremen	Arden, self	Dec. 15th – 22nd
8. Customer Appreciation and Awards Banquet	Alice, Robin, self	Nov. 22nd
9. Prepare or plan a motivational program	Ted, self	Nov. 22nd
10. Review individual goals and objectives for the year	All key people individually	Dec. 15th – 21st

REVIEW OF BUSINESS PLAN

Write how you intend to (1) communicate your business plan to employees, (2) monitor the plan, (3) revise the plan, and (4) measure its success. This can be done with quarterly meetings.

CHAPTER 9
THE BIG PICTURE

In summary, let your business plan become the "play book" that guides your company toward the goals you have set just as the football quarterback uses his play book to guide his team toward the goal line.

Sometimes we just cannot see the "big picture." What is the "big picture"? What does it mean? Try to look at your company as a whole, and not in parts. It means taking a step back and looking at your company decisions, not just in the short term, but consider the total effects of them and how they play out in the long run. It's like a puzzle with lots of pieces. Put them all together and you see the big picture!

On occasion we cannot see this as we get so engrossed with detail we lose sight of the overall situation. Attention to detail is paramount to success, and as managers we must learn to delegate. There must be an overall plan—one that is reviewed on a consistent basis and encompasses all the parts for the good of the whole organization.

As a student of the human anatomy, I have always been impressed with the multiple functions of the human body and the dependence that each part has on the others for survival. The heart, lungs, liver, stomach, skin, etc. all have specific functions that keep the body alive and well. All are fed by a blood supply interwoven throughout the body by veins, arteries, and capillaries. This complex machine takes orders from the brain.

The human body is indeed a work of art, a phenomena beyond compare. However, if any of the vital organs get diseased or seriously impaired, it spells trouble for the whole body. Fortunately, the brain gets this message early on in the form of pain or discomfort. This is called "feedback." If we wear shoes that are too tight, we get blisters. If we stay out in the sun too long, we get burned. It is rare that we have bodily problems without some warning.

Make the comparison that your company is the body and you are the brain. Do you get feedback when there is a problem? You probably get some but very little. The brain has nerve endings that are very sensitive. What do you have? Are you in touch with your staff and customers? Are you walking in their shoes? Many times we are aware of problems, but we procrastinate or put the problem on the back burner hoping it will just go away.

Obviously, a game plan for your business is necessary for its progression and success. The idea of a plan can be extended over into your personal life as well. This does not suggest that you cannot be spontaneous with your approach to life. It only means that a general plan with short-term and long-term objectives can make life easier and more pleasant. This plan should be reviewed on a regular basis just as your business plan is reviewed. Your long-range plan should call for the continuation of your business after you have retired, and even after your death. It should include the key people that play the key roles after your departure whether they are employees or family members.

Do you have a game plan for your life? To quote Shakespeare's Macbeth, "Life is but a walking shadow, a poor player that struts and frets his hour upon the stage, and then is heard no more." Isn't that a sad commentary for one's life? Isn't it true that life is short, but without a plan it's even shorter and with less meaning and satisfaction?

Do you have a plan for your physical health? Does it include a daily exercise program, a proper diet, no smoking, and moderation of food and drink? Is there a plan for your spiritual life? Do you have a plan for your family in case of your death?

It is my earnest desire that you accepted the challenge put forth in the early part of the book. I hope you not only read the book, but participated in it as well. As a result, I trust you are excited about the possibilities that can arise from having a game plan. I hope you will begin to "manage like a quarterback" with a specific play in mind at all times.

Hopefully, *Quarterback Management* has shown you the importance of hiring the right people, playing them in the proper positions for which they are best suited, the importance of an ongoing training program, challenging and motivating your employees to be the best they can be, and the importance of communicating with them your mutual goals and expectations.

Solicit help from your personnel when planning the future of your company and you will find them more supportive and committed.

Believe in your game plan and believe in yourself. Leaders prioritize by doing the most unpleasant tasks first. True leaders are courageous. As you begin to lead with a plan, you will see enormous change. This new attitude will be infectious and contagious with your personnel and with your customers. Your company image will be more positive and the "snowball" effect will impact with more opportunities. Managing will become fun. You will be able to think on a larger scale and attain goals beyond your own expectations. To quote the late Vince Lombardi: "Winning is not a sometime thing; it's an all the time thing. You don't win once in a while; you don't do things right once in a while; you do them right all the time. Winning is a habit. Unfortunately so is losing."

During my high school years I worked for my dad in the summertime building houses. The job involved doing everything from mixing concrete in a portable mixer (dumping one-hundred-pound bags of granular cement, shoveling sand, shoveling crushed rock, and adding water in the mixer). Then this soupy cement was poured into a wheelbarrow and pushed to its final destination (footings, garage floor, sidewalk, etc.). There were many other chores, such as wooden flooring, stud walls, sheet rock, siding, and roofing, but none as hard as that concrete work. I tried every aspect of it and none were easy. My dad would say, "If I worked you as hard as Honey Johnson (my football coach) does, you would think I was a mean man."

The thing I liked most about football was the competition. I just loved to compete and did not like losing at all. But as the years of playing went by, I began to like football because it mimics life itself. Football is an individual commitment to a group effort. It builds character through hard work, sacrifice, respect, leadership, enthusiasm, and most of all decision making. Life is all about making good decisions. You have options in life every day just as a football team has options on every play. The ball is in your hands!

Is this quixotic or unrealistic thinking? No, it isn't. Don't just go through life hoping for the best. Hope is an excuse for doing nothing. You can enjoy the benefits of a better life if you will make the commitment to develop a game plan for your organization and your personal life.

DON'T GO TO BED TONIGHT WITHOUT A GAME PLAN FOR TOMORROW!

About the Author

Van W. Cuthrell was an all-conference high school quarterback in Elizabeth City, North Carolina, starting quarterback at Guilford College in Greensboro, North Carolina, and high school coach for four years in Murfreesboro, North Carolina.

In his business career Cuthrell became president of a Murfreesboro company representing Butler Manufacturing Company's Agri-Products Division. This involved selling grain bins and farm buildings in North Carolina and Virginia. Cuthrell enjoyed enormous success, becoming one of Butler's top five dealerships in the nation, and leading the sale of farmstead buildings year after year.

Cuthrell married his college sweetheart Linda. After his first retirement in 1987, he and Linda spent a year on their sailboat, touring the East Coast north to Maine and then south to the Bahamas. They moved to Raleigh, North Carolina, in 1991 where Cuthrell became a consultant for a commercial building company, Steel Dynamics, Inc. In 1995 he became an owner and was elected president of the firm. After enjoying many more years growing the business with his partners, he retired in 2003.